THE CREATIVE BOOK OF

Flower
Fragrance

THE CREATIVE BOOK OF

Flower Fragrance

Joanna Sheen

LONGMEADOW
PRESS

ISBN 0-681-00727-3

First Longmeadow Press Edition

1 3 5 7 9 0 8 6 4 2

Longmeadow Press and the colophon are
registered trademarks.

CREDITS

Managing Editor: Jane Struthers

Art Director: Roger Daniels

Editor: Felicity Jackson

Photographer: Sue Atkinson, assisted by Kirsty Wilson

Indexer: William Martin

Typeset by: BMD Graphics, Hemel Hempstead

Colour origination by: Regent Publishing Services

Printed in Belgium by: Proost International Book Division

CONTENTS

INTRODUCTION

One of the most important ingredients of any natural thing is its smell – flowers and mosses, trees and grass, everything has its own special fragrance. The smell of the sea can remind you of many happy days on the beach – even the smell of animals can bring back memories of the countryside. The perfume contained in flowers is the strongest and most important of all the natural smells and cannot be prized too highly.

These fragrances can vary from the simple scents like those of honeysuckle and jasmine to the headier aromas of old roses and hyacinths. Everyone has their favourites – bluebells in the spring or autumn leaves and moss, all have a particular place in the palette of flower fragrances that you can collect and blend together.

This book is a collection of ideas to help you use the natural scents of Nature. With a little help from you, they can become exotic creams and perfumes, heady pot pourris and soothing teas and tisanes. Wherever possible, you should aim to use natural products and avoid anything that has unnecessary chemicals in it – but, most of all, enjoy playing with Nature's products.

Many of the ideas featured in this book can be made as treats for yourself but they also make excellent gifts and once your friends and relations have tried some of your special concoctions you will find yourself in great demand!

— DRYING HERBS AND FLOWERS —

M any of the ideas contained in this book use dried herbs, flowers and leaves, and there are various ways in which these ingredients can be preserved. The method you choose will depend partly on personal preference and also on which particular project you are making.

DRYING IN THE MICROWAVE

Many households have a microwave oven now and this can be a very quick and useful way to dry small quantities of herbs and flowers for culinary purposes or for making cosmetics or pot pourri. Drying plant material quickly in the microwave does not enhance its shape and, therefore, is not recommended when you want the material for decorative use.

Lay a sheet of absorbent kitchen paper in the bottom of the microwave oven and place a small bunch of herbs or flowers on the paper. Experiment with different settings and timings, but to start with try a medium setting for 2 minutes. The plant material must be completely dry; if it is not then microwave for a little while longer. Microwave ovens vary from model to model, so it is difficult to give exact timings – a little experimentation on your part will soon tell you how long you need in your particular oven. Keep checking the herbs or flowers to see if they are dry, as they can swiftly turn from thoroughly dried plant material to a pile of desiccated cinders!

AIR DRYING

The oldest and simplest way of preserving plants is to make small bunches and fasten them with an elastic band. It is important to use an elastic band rather than string, otherwise when the stems dry out and shrink, the bunch will disintegrate and end up on the floor. Gather a small bunch, secure with an elastic band approximately 2.5-5 cm (1-2 in) down the stems and hang in a dry, airy position. Many people dry bunches of herbs in their kitchen – the suitability of your kitchen will depend upon how much light and steam affects the area where you intend to dry things. Above an Aga or kitchen range can be a very successful place for drying, provided the plants are kept out of the way of the steam from pans on the top of the cooker. Alternatively, any dry, warm corner of the house will suffice.

It will take from a few days to several weeks to dry the flowers or herbs, depending upon the variety and where they have been hung to dry. Once you are sure they are completely dry, wrap them loosely in tissue paper and store in a suitable box. A long flower box from the florist is ideal if you first cover the holes that serve as handles each end, so that your precious stores are not invaded by insects or mice. It is important to keep your dried flowers or herbs in a reasonably warm, constant atmosphere. A garage is fine in a warm climate or a hot summer but should be used as a very last resort at any other time of year because it is likely to be too damp.

DRYING PETALS AND SMALL ITEMS

To dry individual petals or small items like cones, spread them out on a wire rack used for cooling cakes and leave them in a warm room or, better still, a warm airing cupboard, until they are completely dry. They should then be stored in an airtight container in a dry atmosphere.

GROWING INGREDIENTS IN YOUR GARDEN

Many of the ingredients used in this book can be grown in small gardens or even in window boxes. Growing herbs can be a very rewarding pastime, as you can enjoy the plants in the garden and also your cookery and other hobbies, such as making your own cosmetics, will be much more interesting. Alternatively, larger supermarkets now sell fresh herbs, which you can dry, and it is worth looking around local health food stores as they may have many of the ingredients that are needed.

INGREDIENTS AND CONTAINERS

Many of the items used in this book may well be lying around at home, or you might be able to find suitable substitutes. The suppliers listed at the back of the book will be able to provide the more specialised ingredients if you can't track them down locally. If you are making a special present it is worth using the best possible ingredients: having expended all that effort in making something, it would be a shame to spoil the effect because of a small economy in the ingredients or the container. It is important, for example, to ensure you buy essential oils and not inferior ones that have been blended with carrier oils so they are less strongly scented.

—ROSEMARY HERBAL CUSHION—

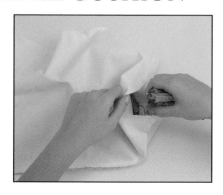

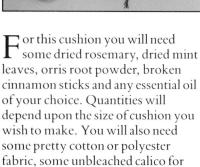

F or this cushion you will need some dried rosemary, dried mint leaves, orris root powder, broken cinnamon sticks and any essential oil of your choice. Quantities will depend upon the size of cushion you wish to make. You will also need some pretty cotton or polyester fabric, some unbleached calico for the liner and some ribbon or lace for decoration.

Make a plain bag slightly smaller than the size of cushion you require using the calico and fill with the mixture of herbs and orris root powder with added drops of essential oil. Cut out 2 pieces of the cotton or polyester material the size you require for the cushion.

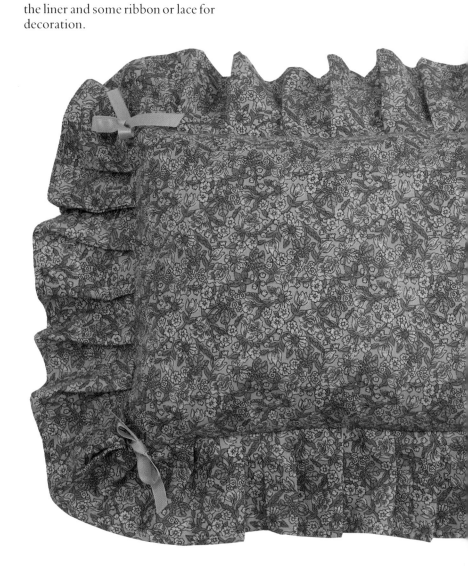

Cut out 10 cm (4 in) strips of the same fabric and join them together to make a frill. Hem one edge.

Place the 2 pieces of cushion fabric right sides together, and pin the raw edge of the frill around 3 sides of the cushion between the 2 pieces of fabric, gathering the frill as you pin. Leave a short side open for turning, pinning the frill to what will be the top side of the cushion.

Sew the frill and fabric together either by hand or machine. Turn the cushion the right way out, place the calico bag inside, then sew up the fourth side. Trim the cushion with ribbon and/or lace as required.

F or the cushion filling you need a
collection of dried flower petals
or some ready-made pot pourri,
mixed with 30 ml (2 tbsp) orris root
powder. The cushion takes two
37.5 cm (15 in) circles of cotton
fabric, a 22.5 cm (9 in) circle of lace
fabric and enough pre-gathered lace
to trim the cushion and the lace
centre. The trimmings from the
cotton fabric can be used for the frill.

Cut a 20 cm (8 in) wide hole from
the centre of one piece of the cotton
fabric.

Back this hole with the circle of lace
fabric, pinning and then sewing it on
firmly.

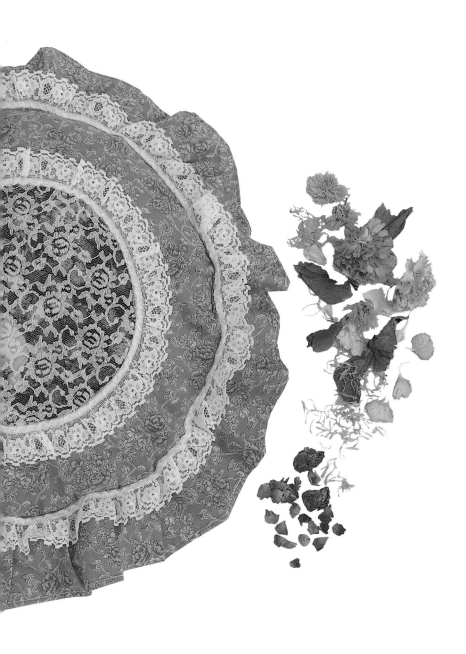

Edge this cut-out section with pre-
gathered lace, then edge this piece of
the cotton fabric with more lace.
Sew 10 cm (4 in) strips of the cotton
fabric together to make a frill.
With right sides together, sew the
2 cushion pieces together with the
frill between them, leaving a gap.
Turn the right way out, pour in the
flower petals, then sew up the gap.

This pillow is made from unbleached calico. You will also need some cotton lace to trim the pillow and some dried hop flowers. Cut 2 pieces of calico and pin them together with the lace edging between them. Pin around 3 of the 4 sides, leaving one open to fill with hops. On the fourth side, pin and then sew the lace to what will be the top side of the pillow.

Turn the pillow the right way out and fill well with hop flowers, shaking them down as you put them into the pillow. Sew up the fourth side.

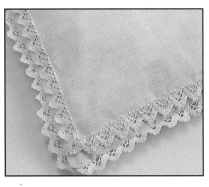

Add an extra row of lace to decorate the pillow, as shown here, if wished. To use, tuck this sleep pillow inside your normal pillow case.

—BAG FOR A LINEN CUPBOARD—

Cut out a rectangle of fabric 50 x 27.5 cm (20 x 11in) and a second circular piece about 12.5 cm (5 in) in diameter. You will also need lace and wide and narrow ribbons. For the filling, collect some dried lavender, rosemary, orange peel and wormwood – all of which will help to scent and protect your linen.

Stitch the lace to one long end of the fabric, adding a ribbon loop at the centre. Sew the wide ribbon about 5 cm (2 in) in from the lace edge, at the top and bottom so ribbon can be threaded through it. Fold the material in half, right sides inwards, and sew the 2 short sides together. Gather the fabric at the base edge to fit it onto the wrong side of the fabric circle. Stitch the circle to the base.

Turn the bag the right way out. Make neat holes where the wide ribbon is joined at the seams, and at the front of the bag. Thread some narrow ribbon through the wide ribbon at the top of the bag. Fill the bag with the rosemary mixture, pull the ribbon to close it and tie the ribbon in a bow. Decorate, if wished, with small ribbon roses and more ribbon.

-BERGAMOT & ORANGE SACHET-

Collect together some dried orange peel, small dried green leaves, 10 ml (2 tsp) orris root powder and some bergamot essential oil. You will also need a 25-27.5 cm (10-11 in) circle of lace fabric edged with pre-gathered lace and some narrow ribbon.

In a bowl, mix together the orange peel, leaves, orris root powder and a few drops of bergamot oil. Make sure all the oil is absorbed by the powder and other ingredients.

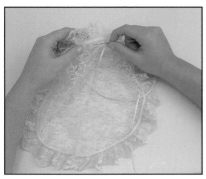

Thread the narrow ribbon all around the edge of the lace circle, about 2.5 cm (1 in) in from the edge.

Pull the ribbon to gather the edges into a bag shape and fill with pot pourri. Gather the ribbon tightly to secure the pot pourri in the sachet and tie in a firm bow.

─── ORANGE & ROSE BATH OIL ───

Pour 75 ml (2½ fl oz/⅓ cup) almond oil into a pretty bottle or container.

Mix together 15 ml (1 tbsp) neroli (orange blossom) essential oil and 5 ml (1 tsp) rose essential oil and add to the bottle.

Shake the bottle well, label clearly and then leave for 2 weeks before using in your bath. Use about 15 ml (1 tbsp) in a bath, adding it to the filled bath.

-ROSE GERANIUM BUBBLE BATH-

I n a small jug, mix together 150 ml (5 fl oz/⅔ cup) any organic washing up liquid, and 150 ml (5 fl oz/⅔ cup) distilled water.

Add 5 ml (1 tsp) rose geranium essential oil to this mixture and stir well.

Add 3 drops of pink food colouring, or more if you want a stronger colour, and mix through the liquid. Decant the bubble bath into an attractive container which can be decorated with ribbons or flowers if it is to be given as a gift. Use 15 ml (1 tbsp) in a bath, adding it to the running water.

I n a bowl, mix together 45 g (1½ oz) dried marjoram, 45 g (1½ oz) dried rosemary, 30 ml (2 tbsp) porridge oats and 15 g (1 tbsp) dried chopped orange peel.

Cut out several 22.5 cm (9 in) circles of calico and place about 20 ml (2 dessertspoons) of the herb mixture in the centre of each one. Gather up the material to make a bag and secure each one with a small elastic band.

Tie long pieces of ribbon around the neck of each bundle, both to decorate and to attach the bag to the bath taps. The bag should be fixed to the taps before you run your bath, so the water runs through the herbal mixture.

—LILY & LEMON BATH BAGS—

Thickly peel 1 or 2 lemons, until you have about 15 g (½ oz) of peel, then chop it roughly. You also need peeled and chopped fresh root ginger, 25 g (1 oz/⅓ cup) porridge oats and some lily of the valley essential oil.

In a bowl, combine all the ingredients, adding 2–3 drops of the lily of the valley oil. Stir well to ensure all the ingredients are well mixed.

Cut out several 25 cm (10 in) circles of calico and place about 20 ml (2 dessertspoons) of the mixture in the centre of each circle. Gather up the material to make a bag and secure with a small elastic band. Tie long pieces of ribbon around the neck of each bundle, both to decorate and to attach the bag to the bath taps, so the water runs through the mixture.

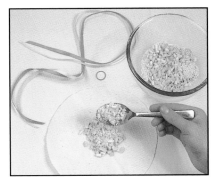

——— HONEYSUCKLE BATH OIL ———

P ut 115 ml (4 fl oz/½ cup) castor oil in a jug and add 10 drops honeysuckle perfume or pot pourri oil. Mix well.

Choose some suitable containers – whether you are making this as a gift or for yourself, it always looks much better in an attractive container. Pour the mixture into the containers.

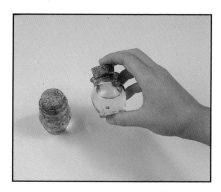

Seal well and label. About 5 ml (1 tsp) is sufficient for an average bath. Add it to the filled bath.

LAVENDER FOOT BATH

P ut 450 ml (16 fl oz/2 cups) lavender flowers and leaves in a small saucepan and add 300 ml (10 fl oz/ 1¼ cups) water.

Heat to simmering point and then simmer gently for about 5 minutes, stirring occasionally.

Let the contents of the pan cool and then strain through a fine sieve into a jug. Pour the liquid into a bottle. When a soothing foot bath is required, add half the bottle to a bowl of warm water and soak the feet well.

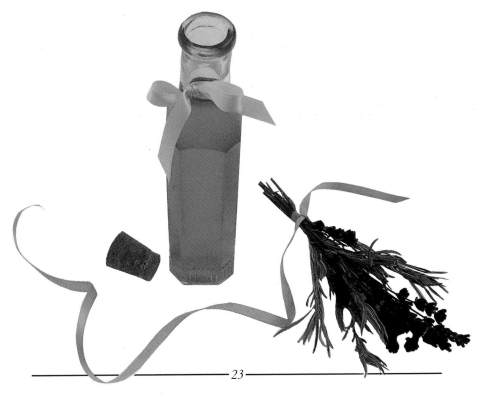

Put 45 ml (3 tbsp) bicarbonate of soda in a bowl and add 12 drops sweet orange or neroli (orange blossom) essential oil and 6 drops strawberry perfume or pot pourri oil. Mix well together.

Add some pink food colouring – 3 drops should be ample, depending on the depth of colour required.

Mix the food colouring in well, which takes quite a while and needs to be done very thoroughly. Pour the salts into a clear jar and decorate with a pink ribbon. Add about 15 ml (1 tbsp) to a hot bath.

ROSE WATER

Put 15 g (½ oz) dried red rose petals in a bowl. Scented petals are best but as rose oil is being added later, they are not essential.

Pour 300 ml (10 fl oz/1¼ cups) boiling water over the petals and stir well. Leave to infuse for roughly 2 hours.

Strain the liquid through a fine sieve into a jug or bowl, pressing the petals hard to extract every drop of rose water possible, then add 2 drops of rose essential oil. Pour the finished mixture into a bottle, seal and label clearly. Use the rose water as a cologne to refresh, as a toner for dry skin or add to washing water.

Put 45 ml (3 tbsp) dried strawberry leaves in a heatproof bowl. Bring just over 100 ml (3½ fl oz/⅓ cup) distilled water to the boil, then pour over the strawberry leaves. Leave to infuse for 4–5 hours.

Heat 115 ml (4 fl oz/½ cup) rose water in a bowl set over a saucepan of simmering water. When hot, add 5 ml (1 tsp) borax.

Stir very gently until the borax has completely dissolved.

Remove the bowl from the heat. Strain the liquid away from the strawberry leaves through a sieve into the rose water and borax mixture.

Pour the liquid into a suitable bottle. This aftershave works best if it is kept cool or, better still, stored in the refrigerator before and after use.

BERGAMOT COLOGNE

This is a delicious after-bath cologne. You will need some cheap vodka, distilled water, dried orange peel, cloves, a fresh rose and a carnation, and bergamot essential oil.

Take a fresh rose and a fresh carnation and strip off the petals, placing them in a screw-top jar. Pour over 115 ml (4 fl oz/½ cup) cheap vodka. Screw on the top, shake well and leave on a sunny windowsill for about 1 week.

Measure 45 ml (3 tbsp) dried orange peel and 5 ml (1 tsp) cloves into a bowl and pour over 350 ml (12 fl oz/ 1½ cups) boiling distilled water. Leave to stand for 5-6 hours.

Strain both the flower and vodka mixture and the orange and clove mixture through a fine sieve into a bowl or jug.

Check for clarity – the liquid may need straining through a finer sieve to clear it completely. Add 3 drops bergamot essential oil and stir well. Pour the liquid into a bottle and keep in the refrigerator or other cool place. Use as an after-bath cologne.

Place 15 ml (1 tbsp) fresh mint leaves in a bowl with 15 ml (1 tbsp) rosemary leaves and pour over 50 ml (2 fl oz/¼ cup) cheap vodka.

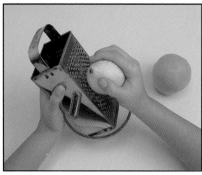

Carefully grate the peel from 1 orange and 1 lemon, removing as much as possible.

Add the orange and lemon peel to the mint, rosemary and vodka mixture.

Add 115 ml (4 fl oz/½ cup) rose water and mix all the ingredients together.

Leave the mixture for about 1 week, stirring vigorously every day. Carefully strain the liquid through a sieve and then pour into a bottle. Keep in a cool place and use as a cologne or in bath water.

ORANGE COLOGNE

P our 150 ml (5 fl oz/⅔ cup) cheap
vodka into a large perfume
bottle or 2 small bottles.

Add 6 drops neroli (orange blossom)
essential oil and 2 drops coriander
essential oil to the vodka.

Shake the bottle or bottles very
vigorously. Leave to stand for 1-2
weeks, then check the fragrance – if
you wish to alter the balance of the
ingredients, add a drop more of
whichever fragrance you require.

P ut 30 ml (2 tbsp) dried rosemary in a heatproof bowl. Heat 200 ml (7 fl oz/¾ cup) distilled water and pour over the dried rosemary. Leave to infuse for 5-6 hours.

Add 5 ml (1 tsp) almond oil and 2 drops rosemary essential oil to the mixture.

Whisk gently until all the ingredients are well mixed. Then strain the liquid through a fine sieve and pour into a bottle. Keep in a cool place.

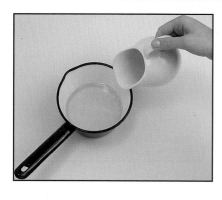

Combine 250 ml (9 fl oz/1 cup) cider vinegar and 250 ml (9 fl oz/ 1 cup) water in a saucepan and heat gently – do not boil.

Remove from the heat and add 15 ml (1 tbsp) dried basil and 15 ml (1 tbsp) dried mint. Leave to infuse for 5-6 hours.

Strain the mixture through a fine sieve and pour into a bottle. Use in the bath – about a cupful for an average bath.

—GERANIUM TOILET VINEGAR—

Combine 550 ml (20 fl oz/2½ cups) cider vinegar with the same quantity of water in a saucepan and heat to boiling point. Put 25 g (1 oz) lavender flowers and 85 g (3 oz) geranium leaves in a heatproof bowl, pour over the boiling liquid and leave to infuse for 10–12 hours.

Strain the liquid from the leaves through a fine sieve, pressing the leaves and lavender down well to extract as much liquid as possible.

Add 2 drops lavender essential oil and 2 drops rose geranium essential oil and mix gently. Pour into bottles. Use in the bath – about a cupful for an average bath.

The paper is scented with a strong perfume that is easily made by making up an extra strong sachet of lavender pot pourri and storing it with the paper and envelopes in a box. Lavender, orris root powder and lavender essential oil are combined to make a very potent sachet which soon imparts its fragrance to the contents of the box of writing paper.

Mix 30 ml (2 tbsp) dried lavender flowers with 5 ml (1 tsp) orris root powder and add 2 or 3 drops lavender essential oil. Mix all these ingredients together carefully with a metal spoon until the oil and orris root powder are well dispersed amongst the lavender flowers.

Cut out one or more 17.5 cm (7 in) circles of net fabric. Place some or all of the mixture onto the circles and tie the bundle or bundles with wire or ribbons. Place the net bundle or bundles in the box in which you intend to store the paper and envelopes and leave for at least a week, longer if possible, and your letters will have an unforgettable fragrance.

——LAVENDER-SCENTED INK——

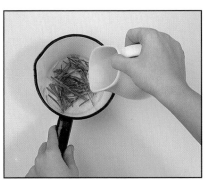

You can add a sophisticated touch to all your correspondence by using an ink that has been scented with dried lavender leaves. If you combine this with scented paper and envelopes, your letter will definitely smell delicious! You need a handful of fresh or dried lavender leaves, a bottle of ink and some water.

Place the lavender leaves in a small saucepan and add approximately 115 ml (4 fl oz/½ cup) water. Bring the water to the boil, then turn the heat down as low as possible and simmer gently for about 30 minutes. Keep an eye on the pan and do not allow the water to evaporate completely. If it gets too low, then add a little more.

Once the mixture is brown and has become strongly scented, strain off the liquid and discard the lavender leaves. Add a small amount of the liquid to the ink until you are happy with the strength of smell. Here the lavender liquid has been added to lavender-coloured ink to complete the effect.

SANTOLINA INSECT DETERRENT

For this insect deterrent you need 685 ml (24 fl oz/3 cups) dried santolina or cotton lavender and 25 g (1 oz) each of cloves, caraway and mace. You will also need 2 or 3 cinnamon sticks.

Crush the cinnamon sticks into all the other ingredients in a bowl and mix well.

Cut out several 25 cm (10 in) circles of calico and fill each one with 15 ml (1 tbsp) of the mixture. Gather up the sides and tie with string or twine. Place in any cupboards or areas that you need to keep insect-free.

—LAVENDER MOTH REPELLENT—

In a bowl, mix together 55 g (2 oz) each of dried rosemary, lavender and wormwood.

Add to the mixture 25 g (1 oz/¼ cup) orris root powder, 2 crushed cinnamon sticks and 10 ml (2 tsp) cloves and mix well.

Add 3 drops lavender essential oil and 1 drop rosemary essential oil. Mix well, then place 15 ml (1 tbsp) of the mixture in the centre of a lace-edged handkerchief. Gather up the sides and secure with a small elastic band. Repeat to make as many as you need. Hang in wardrobes or a linen cupboard with a loop of ribbon.

This eyebath used cold from the refrigerator will calm sore eyes and bring a sparkle back to tired eyes. You need 7 g (¼ oz) dried cornflowers and 200 ml (7 fl oz/scant 1 cup) distilled water.

Put the cornflowers in a heatproof bowl. Bring the distilled water to the boil and pour it over the cornflowers. Leave to infuse for 1 hour.

Strain carefully through a fine sieve into a jug or bottle. Chill in the refrigerator. To refresh eyes, soak pads of cotton wool with this mixture, place on closed eyes and rest for 15–20 minutes. This mix should be used fresh and only stored for a maximum of 24 hours in the refrigerator.

-LAVENDER FURNITURE POLISH-

I nto a screw-top jar, pour 150 ml (5 fl oz/⅔ cup) turpentine, 150 ml (5 fl oz/⅔ cup) linseed oil, 85 ml (3 fl oz/⅓ cup) cider vinegar and 85 ml (3 fl oz/⅓ cup) methylated spirits.

Add 10-12 drops lavender essential oil to the ingredients in the jar.

Screw on the lid and shake really thoroughly. Use the mixture to feed wood and always polish off well to give a really good shine to furniture.

In a bowl mix together 250 ml (9 fl oz/1 cup) each of the following: dried lavender flowers, dried thyme, dried oregano and dried orange peel.

Add 1 bottle of white wine (not a special vintage!)

Stir really well until the wine is completely incorporated.

Cover with cling film and leave in a warm room for 1–2 weeks. Then strain the liquid and pour into a bottle. Add 10–15 ml (2–3 tsp) to a final rinse when hand–washing clothes or use as a final rinse for your hair.

This face mask is good for oily skins. In a bowl, whisk 2 egg whites until they are standing in soft peaks.

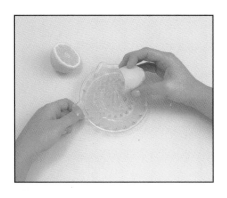

Squeeze half a lemon and measure out 5 ml (1 tsp) of juice. Chop 1 cucumber into cubes.

Put the egg whites in a food processor or blender with 3 ice cubes, the lemon juice, chopped cucumber, 5 ml (1 tsp) vodka and 4 drops peppermint essential oil. Blend until a smooth paste is formed.

To use, apply the mixture to your face, leave for 5-10 minutes, then rinse off carefully. Any remaining mixture may be stored in the refrigerator for a day or so.

RASPBERRY & ORANGE INFUSION

Put 15 ml (1 tbsp) dried raspberry leaves with the same quantity of strawberry leaves and dried orange peel in a large bowl.

Pour over 2 litres (70 fl oz/9 cups) boiling water.

Add 1–2 drops sweet orange or neroli (orange blossom) essential oil. Stir well until all the ingredients are mixed together. To use, place a towel over your head, lower your face until it is just above the bowl and breathe in the vapour. Stay under the towel for about 10 minutes, then use a gentle astringent to close the pores.

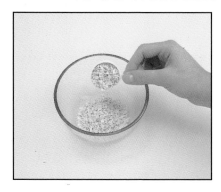

Measure 4.5 ml (3 tbsp) porridge oats into a bowl. If you prefer a finer mask, process the porridge oats in a food processor or blender for a few seconds first.

Add 15–30 ml (1–2 tbsp) rose water, depending on the preferred consistency, working the mixture into a paste.

Add 2 drops rose essential oil and mix in thoroughly. To use, apply to the face and leave for 15 minutes, then rinse off gently. Apply a gentle toner to close the pores. This is a good refining mask.

I n a bowl, mix together 45 ml
(3 tbsp) dried red rose petals, 15 ml
(1 tbsp) dried raspberry leaves and
5 ml (1 tsp) camomile flowers.

Heat 150 ml (5 fl oz/⅔ cup) distilled
water with 45 ml (3 tbsp) cider
vinegar but do not allow it to boil.
Pour the hot liquid over the flowers
and leaves.

Stir the mixture well and leave to
cool. When cold, cover with cling
film and leave in the refrigerator for
1 week.

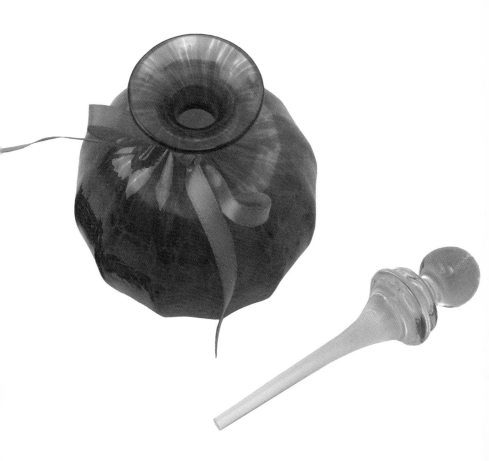

Strain the liquid away from the petals through a fine sieve into a bowl.

In a small bowl, mix together 5 ml (1 tsp) borax and 200 ml (7 fl oz/ ¾ cup) rose water. Add to the rose and raspberry liquid and mix really well. Then pour into a bottle and label clearly. This facial splash feels nicest if used straight from the refrigerator.

Collect some roses fresh from the garden or, if necessary, buy some from a good florist, checking that they have not been sprayed with chemicals. You will also need 45 ml (3 tbsp) porridge oats, 15 ml (1 tbsp) single (light) cream, 30 ml (2 tbsp) almond oil and some rose water.

Remove the petals from the roses and chop them finely or process them in a food processor. Then fill a measuring jug with the petals, packing them down quite hard until you reach the 200 ml (7 fl oz/¾ cup) level.

Add the porridge oats, then chop the mixture even more finely or re-process in the food processor.

Place the chopped ingredients in a bowl and add the single (light) cream and almond oil. Mix these in thoroughly.

Finally, add a little rose water until the mixture is a workable paste. To use, apply the mask and leave on the face for 20-30 minutes whilst you relax, then gently rinse off.

—ELDERFLOWER ASTRINGENT—

Put 10 ml (2 tsp) dried elderflowers in a heatproof bowl. Heat 1 litre (35 fl oz/4½ cups) distilled water and pour it over the dried elderflowers. Cover with cling film and leave to infuse for about 3–4 hours.

Strain the liquid away from the flowers through a fine sieve. Warm 30 ml (2 tbsp) white vinegar and dissolve 1.25 ml (¼ tsp) borax in the vinegar.

Add the vinegar and borax mixture to the elderflower liquid and mix well. Pour into a bottle and keep in a cool place – it is best used straight from the refrigerator and is ideal for oily skins.

MARIGOLD MASK

For this mask you must use dried marigold petals (any variety) and a good quality plain yoghurt, made from either sheep's or cow's milk. Put 90 ml (6 tbsp) dried marigold petals in a bowl. Heat 45 ml (3 tbsp) distilled water and then pour it over the petals.

Add 60 ml (4 tbsp) oatmeal and 15 ml (1 tbsp) granulated lecithin. Stir the mixture very vigorously.

Add 60 ml (4 tbsp) plain yoghurt and mix in well. The mask should be applied to your face whilst it is still warm. Leave the mask on for 20–30 minutes and then carefully rinse it off with lukewarm water.

M elt 15 ml (1 tbsp) lanolin in a bowl set over a saucepan with 2.5-5 cm (1–2 in) of simmering water in it.

Once the lanolin has melted, remove from the heat and add 175 ml (6 fl oz/ ¾ cup) almond oil and mix gently.

Add 250 ml (9 fl oz/1 cup) dried elderflowers and stir in. Place the bowl and pan of hot water back on the heat and let the water simmer very gently for about 20 minutes.

Strain the mixture through a sieve, then pour it into a jar and let it cool. This is an excellent all-purpose hand or body cream.

-POPPY & CORNFLOWER LOTION-

This lotion is ideal for the area around the eyes. It is gentle enough for dry skin and helps to tighten the areas of the face most prone to wrinkles. You need 30 ml (2 tbsp) dried poppy petals, 15 ml (1 tbsp) dried cornflowers, 300 ml (10 fl oz/1¼ cups) distilled water and a suitable bottle or container and some ribbon.

Place the poppy petals and cornflowers in a small saucepan and add the distilled water. Bring to the boil and then turn off the heat. Allow the petals to infuse for 30-40 minutes.

Strain the infusion through a fine sieve or tea strainer into a jug. Pour the liquid from the jug into your chosen bottle or bottles and seal. Use this mixture by applying it, on a pad of cotton wool, to the face and neck both night and morning. It is best kept in the refrigerator, as this helps to preserve the mixture and also makes the lotion feel extra invigorating when it is applied.

ORANGE FLOWER NIGHT CREAM

This is a wonderfully rich and nourishing cream that is ideal for softening dry skin at night. You need 10 ml (2 tsp) lanolin, 10 ml (2 tsp) beeswax (or some small pieces from a sheet), 20 ml (4 tsp) almond oil, 15 ml (3 tsp) distilled water, a pinch of borax, 4 capsules wheatgerm oil and 3–4 drops neroli (orange blossom) essential oil. Any container with a tight-fitting lid is suitable.

Put the lanolin, beeswax and almond oil in a bowl and place over a saucepan containing 2.5–5 cm (1–2 in) of water. Heat the water and gently melt the ingredients, stirring carefully.

Heat the distilled water in a separate pan, then pour it over the borax to dissolve it and pour into the oil mixture. Stir well, then pierce the capsules of wheatgerm oil and add the contents to the cream. Add the neroli essential oil and mix in thoroughly. Spoon into a container before the mixture becomes too cool and sets. This cream should be used nightly for the best results.

P ut 215 ml (7½ fl oz/¾ cup plus 8 tsp) almond oil in a heatproof bowl set over a saucepan of simmering water, add 30 ml (2 tbsp) beeswax and stir until melted.

Add 15 ml (1 tbsp) glycerine to the mixture and stir well.

Warm 175 ml (6 fl oz/¾ cup) rose water, add 5 ml (1 tsp) borax and stir until dissolved, then add to the beeswax mixture.

Remove the bowl of beeswax mixture from the saucepan and whisk really well until the mixture has cooled. Spoon into a jar and keep this mixture in the refrigerator.

——LAVENDER MOISTURISER——

P ut 45 ml (3 tbsp) lanolin and 115 ml (4 fl oz/½ cup) beeswax in a heatproof bowl set over a saucepan with 2.5-5 cm (1-2 in) simmering water in it. Stir until the beeswax has melted.

Add 175 ml (6 fl oz/¾ cup) almond oil and whisk all the ingredients together.

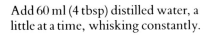

Add 60 ml (4 tbsp) distilled water, a little at a time, whisking constantly.

Remove the bowl from the saucepan and whisk in 10 drops lavender essential oil, 10 drops sweet orange essential oil, 5 drops rosemary essential oil and 5 drops bergamot essential oil. Spoon into suitable containers and keep cool.

ROSEHIP FACE LOTION

Put 60 ml (4 tbsp) crushed rosehips in a heatproof bowl. In a small saucepan, bring 200 ml (7 fl oz/ ¾ cup) distilled water to the boil. Pour over the rosehips and leave to infuse for 1–2 hours.

Strain the liquid away from the rosehips by pouring it through some muslin or cheesecloth into another bowl.

Heat 20 ml (4 tsp) almond oil in a bowl set over a saucepan with 2.5–5 cm (1–2 in) simmering water in the bottom. Add 10 ml (2 tsp) granulated lecithin and stir well until the granules have dissolved.

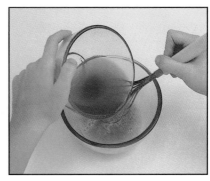

Add 5 ml (1 tsp) cider vinegar to the rosehip water. Set the bowl over a saucepan of simmering water and heat gently almost to boiling point – do not allow to boil.

Mix all the ingredients together and whisk well until they have cooled. Pour the lotion into a bottle and keep in the refrigerator.

TRADITIONAL ROSE POT POURRI

I n a large bowl, mix together
450 ml (16 fl oz/2 cups) dried red
rose petals, 250 ml (9 fl oz/1 cup)
lavender and 115 ml (4 fl oz/½ cup)
dried marjoram. Add 15 ml (1 tbsp)
cloves, 115 ml (4 fl oz/½ cup) dried
orange peel and 6 nutmegs. Break
3-4 cinnamon sticks into the mixture
as well.

Stir all the ingredients well, then add
45 ml (3 tbsp) orris root powder.

Add 15 ml (1 tbsp) of any rose pot
pourri oil and stir well – use a metal
spoon rather than a wooden one as
wood absorbs the oil. When the oil is
well mixed in, place the mixture in a
plastic bag and seal. Leave to mature
for 2 weeks, shaking occasionally,
and then turn into a bowl to display.

ORANGE & CARROT MOISTURISER

Melt 5 ml (1 tsp) beeswax with 15 ml (1 tbsp) lanolin and 90 ml (6 tbsp) almond oil in a bowl set over a saucepan of simmering water. Stir gently while they are melting.

Heat 45 ml (3 tbsp) distilled water with 60 ml (4 tbsp) carrot juice in a small saucepan. Add 2.5 ml (½ tsp) borax and dissolve well.

Add 30 ml (2 tbsp) glycerine to the beeswax and oil mixture and stir well. Remove the bowl from the saucepan and add the carrot juice mixture to the oil mixture, whisking until the cream has cooled down. Add 3 drops sweet orange essential oil to the cream, then spoon into a jar with a tight-fitting lid.

-HERB & LAVENDER POT POURRI-

Place 250 ml (9 fl oz/1 cup) lavender flowers in a bowl and add 115 ml (4 fl oz/½ cup) each of the following: dried mint, marjoram and oregano flowers. Add 250 ml (9 fl oz/1 cup) small green leaves to this mixture.

Mix all these ingredients well and then add 30 ml (2 tbsp) orris root powder.

Finally, add 10 ml (2 tsp) lavender oil, using either essential oil or a pot pourri oil. Mix well with a metal spoon. Place the mixture in a plastic bag and leave to mature for about 2 weeks, shaking regularly. Once matured, display the pot pourri in a suitable container.

The dried apple slices for this pot pourri can be dried in the bottom of the oven on a low temperature for several hours. In a bowl, mix together 250 ml (9 fl oz/ 1 cup) of each of the following: peach stones, rosehips, beech masts, larch cones and star anise. Add 3 or 4 whole or cracked nutmegs and 6 broken cinnamon sticks.

Add to this mixture 60 ml (4 tbsp) orris root powder and mix in well. Add 15 ml (1 tbsp) allspice essential oil and 15 ml (1 tbsp) sweet orange essential oil and mix thoroughly with a metal spoon.

Add 250 ml (9 fl oz/1 cup) dried apple slices. Place the mixture in a plastic bag and leave to mature for about 2 weeks, shaking regularly. Once matured, display the pot pourri in a suitable container.

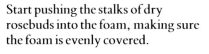

Make a long loop of ribbon and wrap some florist's wire around the base of the loop, leaving a long enough leg to pass through a 7 cm (2¾ in) or 9 cm (3½ in) dried flower foam ball. Pass the wire through the ball until the base of the loop has disappeared. Trim the wire to within 1 cm (½ in) of the ball and bend that 1 cm (½ in) back on itself to disappear inside the foam.

Start pushing the stalks of dry rosebuds into the foam, making sure the foam is evenly covered.

Once the ball is covered with rosebuds, place some cardamom pods between the roses to add an extra colour to the ball, using a hot glue gun to secure them. Then scent the ball with a few drops of rose essential oil.

In a large bowl, mix together 250 ml (9 fl oz/1 cup) dried orange peel and 30 ml (2 tbsp) orris root powder.

Add 15 ml (1 tbsp) sweet orange essential oil and 15 ml (1 tbsp) mixed spice essential oil to this basic mixture.

Mix in 685 ml (24 fl oz/3 cups) assorted cones, acorns etc and stir well. Place all the ingredients in a plastic bag and seal. Leave the mixture for at least 2 weeks, shaking the bag regularly, then display in a pretty basket.

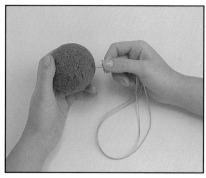

M ake 2 long loops with toning colour ribbons and wrap some florist's wire around the base of the loops, leaving a long enough leg to pass through a 7 cm (2¾ in) or 9 cm (3½ in) dried flower foam ball.

Push the wire through the ball, until the base of each loop has disappeared. Trim the wire to within 1 cm (½ in) of the ball and bend that 1 cm (½ in) back on itself to disappear inside the foam.

Cover the foam ball with sea lavender, or *Statice dumosa*.

Place other dried flowers, such as achillea or helichrysum, at random over the ball. You can also add wired pearl loops or more ribbon loops if you like.

Using a favourite essential oil or pot pourri oil, place a few drops deep into the dried flowers to add a finishing touch.

──ROSE-SCENTED CONFETTI──

Use red rose petals for this confetti – other colours are never as successful. Place 450 ml (16 fl oz/2 cups) dried red rose petals in a large bowl.

Sprinkle over 5 ml (1 tsp) rose essential oil and stir well with a metal spoon.

Place the rose petals in a plastic bag and leave for about 2 weeks, shaking them occasionally.

Once they have matured, transfer the petals to a cellophane bag or bags and secure with some pretty rose-coloured ribbon.

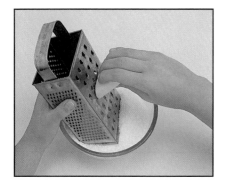

Grate 300 g (10 oz) plain unscented soap into a mixing bowl.

Pour 250 ml (9 fl oz/1 cup) boiling water over the grated soap.

Add 4 drops pink food colouring, 5 drops carnation essential oil and 1 drop clove essential oil.

Mix really thoroughly, using a metal spoon, and leave to harden.

Once the soap has hardened, break off small pieces, the size of a table tennis ball.

Roll into balls of an even size and leave to become even harder. When they are really hard, polish with a piece of cotton wool dipped in carnation essential oil.

──GERANIUM SOAP BALLS──

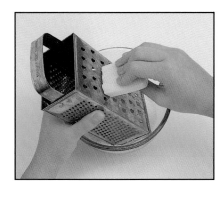

Grate 1 large or 2 small bars of plain unscented soap into a bowl.

Heat 55 ml (2 fl oz/¼ cup) rose water and pour over the grated soap.

Add 2 drops grapefruit essential oil and 2 drops rose geranium essential oil and some lemon yellow food colouring, if desired. Mix in thoroughly.

Let the mixture stand for 1–2 days, then divide into even-sized pieces.

Roll the pieces into smooth balls, allow them to dry thoroughly and then polish them with a piece of cotton wool dipped in rose water.

P ut 75 ml (5 tbsp) lavender flowers
in a food processor or blender
with 30 ml (2 tbsp) dried chopped
mixed herbs and process to a
powder. This is quite a lengthy
process but needs to be done
thoroughly.

In a bowl, combine 75 ml (5 tbsp)
precipitated chalk, 30 ml (2 tbsp) rice
flour and 45 ml (3 tbsp) cornflour.

Add the powdered lavender flowers
and powdered mixed herbs.

Finally, add 15 ml (1 tbsp) lavender essential oil and mix all the ingredients thoroughly before transferring to a suitable container.

—ORANGE & GINGER POWDER—

I n a bowl, combine 45 ml (3 tbsp) cornflour, 30 ml (2 tbsp) rice flour and 75 ml (5 tbsp) precipitated chalk.

Add 30 ml (2 tbsp) ground ginger to the ingredients in the bowl.

Add 15 ml (1 tbsp) neroli (orange blossom) essential oil and mix all the ingredients very thoroughly with a metal spoon. Transfer to an attractive container. Use as talcum powder.

In a bowl, mix together 25 g (1 oz/ ¼ cup) orris root powder with 85 g (3 oz/¾ cup) plain talcum powder.

Add 2 drops rosemary essential oil and 2 drops lemon essential oil. Stir well with a metal spoon.

Once the oils have been well mixed in, use as a freshener between shampoos. Rub a small quantity into the hair and then brush out well with a bristle brush.

ELDERBERRY HAIR RINSE

Put 115 g (4 oz) elderberries in a bowl and crush them slightly.

Bring 550 ml (20 fl oz/2½ cups) water to boiling point and pour over the elderberries.

Stir the mixture and leave to infuse for approximately 2 hours.

Strain off the liquid and pour into a bottle. Used as a final rinse for grey hair, it imparts a slight blue/grey tone.

Put 115 g (4 oz) camomile flowers in a heatproof bowl. Heat 550 ml (20 fl oz/2½ cups) water to boiling point and pour over the camomile flowers. Leave to infuse for 2 hours.

Strain the liquid away from the flowers into a bowl through a fine sieve.

Pour the camomile liquid into a jug, passing it through some muslin to strain off any tiny pieces of camomile left behind. Pour into a pretty container and use as a final rinse when washing blonde hair.

—ORGANDIE BAG WITH NET—

Cut circles of net large enough to enclose the gift you are wrapping. Wrap the net around the gift, secure with fine wire or a small elastic band, then tie with a ribbon bow.

Make a simple bag from a piece of organdie and place the net bundle inside.

Tie the organdie bag with velvet ribbon and decorate with fresh or dried flowers.

−DRAMATIC BLACK LACE WRAP−

Cut out circles of black net large enough to cover the gift you are wrapping. Wrap the net around the gift and secure with some fine wire or a small elastic band.

Decorate the net bundle with some gold cord or ribbon, or pearls tied around the neck.

Make a simple bag from black lace
material, large enough to take the net
bundle.

Place the net bundle inside the lace
bag and decorate with gold cord and/
or pearls.

This is a good way to wrap up a present that is an awkward shape. You will need a purpose-made gift bag in foil paper, some net, fine wire or an elastic band and some ribbons.

Cut out circles of net large enough to enclose the gift you are wrapping. Wrap the net around the gift, overwrapping several times to hide the contents. Secure with fine wire or a small elastic band, then tie with a ribbon bow.

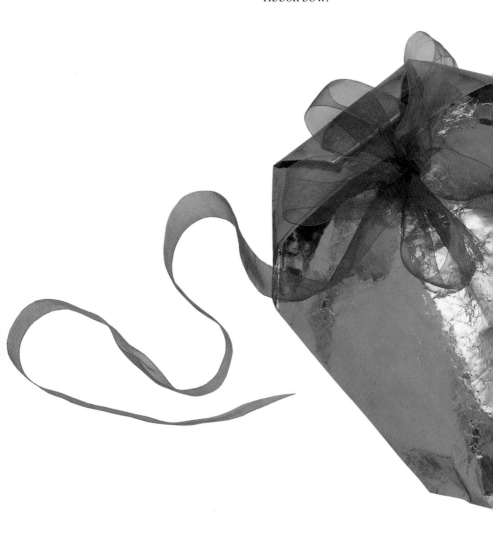

Choose a purpose-made gift bag in foil paper and place the net bundle inside.

Fold over the top of the foil and fasten securely with tape.

Decorate the package with ribbon and/or flowers, if wished.

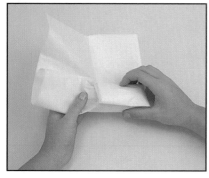

W rap your gift carefully in tissue paper to pad it out to prevent any damage.

Using any lightweight tartan fabric, make a plain bag large enough to hold the gift.

Secure the neck of the bag with an elastic band and then decorate with lace and satin ribbons.

—DECORATIVE NET BUNDLE—

A pretty net bundle is the ideal solution when your gift is a large bottle or jar which can be difficult to wrap. Cut out several circles of net large enough to encase the bottle or jar. Using several different colours of net can be very effective.

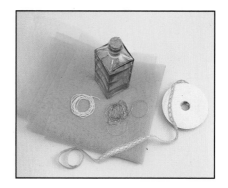

Wrap the net around the bottle or jar and secure very tightly at the neck of the bottle with wire or an elastic band.

Decorate with lace ribbons, or ribbons made from net or chiffon, gold cord and pearls, as wished.

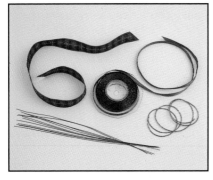

You will need plenty of ribbon, some gold cord if you wish and lengths of fine florist's wire.

Cut a piece of ribbon approximately 30 cm (12 in) long and wrap one end over the other as in the photograph.

Gather the middle of the bow and secure by binding a piece of fine florist's wire around the centre.

Trim off any excess wire once the bow is held securely in shape.

Cover the piece of wire with narrow ribbon that tones with the bow or with gold cord.

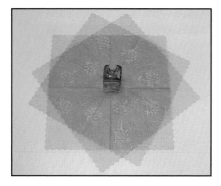

Take 3 or 4 fine Japanese table napkins and place them on top of one another so that the points look like petals. Place the gift you are wrapping in the centre.

Gather up the sides of the napkins and secure them at the neck of the bottle or container with a piece of fine wire.

Finish the package by decorating it with pretty ribbon, gold cord or lace.

INDEX

SUPPLIERS

Pot pourri ingredients, pressed and dried flowers:

Joanna Sheen Limited
PO Box 52, Newton Abbot, Devon TQ12 4YF

Pot pourri and cosmetic ingredients:
Culpeper Limited
21 Bruton Street, London W1X 7DA

Hand-blown glass and scent bottles:
Teign Valley Glass
Pottery Road, Bovey Tracey, Devon TQ13 9DS

PRINTED IN BELGIUM BY

INTERNATIONAL BOOK PRODUCTION